Great Canadian Chronicles: Extraordinary Tales of Resilience, Innovation, and Heritage

Welcome to "Great Canadian Chronicles: Extraordinary Tales of Resilience, Innovation, and Heritage." In this captivating book, we delve into the remarkable stories that have shaped the history and culture of Canada. From the rugged landscapes of the Rocky Mountains to the vibrant multicultural cities, Canada is a nation brimming with tales of triumph, ingenuity, and a deep connection to its heritage.

Within these pages, you will uncover 16 inspiring case studies that highlight the resilience and resourcefulness of Canadians in the face of challenges, the groundbreaking innovations that have transformed industries, and the rich cultural heritage that continues to thrive across the country. Each story is a testament to the indomitable spirit and unwavering determination of the Canadian people.

Prepare to embark on a journey through time and geography as we explore the diverse landscapes, diverse communities, and diverse achievements of Canada. From the iconic figures who have left an indelible mark on the nation's history to the unsung heroes whose contributions have made a significant impact, "Great Canadian Chronicles" celebrates the extraordinary individuals and events that have shaped Canada's identity.

Whether you're a proud Canadian seeking to deepen your connection to the country or an international reader intrigued by the stories of a remarkable nation, this book will take you on an immersive adventure through the annals of Canadian history. Discover the courage, innovation, and cultural richness that define Canada and its people.

Join us as we uncover the hidden gems of Canadian history and showcase the incredible tales that have left an indelible imprint on the fabric of the nation. "Great Canadian Chronicles" invites you to be inspired, informed, and enthralled by the remarkable resilience, innovation, and heritage of Canada and its people. Let the journey begin!

The Story of Terry Fox

Terry Fox was a Canadian athlete and cancer activist who became an inspirational figure for people around the world. Born on July 28, 1958, in Winnipeg, Manitoba, Terry Fox developed a passion for sports from a young age. However, in 1977, at the age of 18, he was diagnosed with osteosarcoma, a form of bone cancer, which resulted in the amputation of his right leg above the knee.

Following his surgery and recovery, Terry Fox was determined to make a difference and raise awareness for cancer research. In 1980, he embarked on a remarkable journey known as the "Marathon of Hope." Terry's goal was to run across Canada, covering a distance of approximately 5,373 kilometers (3,339 miles), to raise funds for cancer research.

Starting in St. John's, Newfoundland, on April 12, 1980, Terry Fox ran an average of 42 kilometers (26 miles) per day, often through challenging weather conditions and physical pain. His indomitable spirit and unwavering determination captured the hearts and minds of Canadians and people worldwide.

Despite the immense challenges he faced, Terry Fox's journey inspired a nation. Communities came together to support him along the route, donating funds to his cause and cheering him on as he made his way across the country. His message of hope, perseverance, and the desire to make a difference resonated with people from all walks of life.

Sadly, Terry Fox's run came to an end on September 1, 1980, near Thunder Bay, Ontario, as the cancer spread to his lungs. Although he was unable to complete his cross-country journey, Terry's legacy lived on. His Marathon of Hope had raised millions of dollars for cancer research and inspired countless individuals to continue his mission.

Terry Fox's courageous fight against cancer and his selfless dedication to raising awareness and funds for cancer research made him a symbol of hope and determination. The annual Terry Fox Run, which takes place in countries around the world, continues to raise funds for cancer research in his honor. Terry's story serves as a reminder of the power of the human spirit and the impact that one person can have on the lives of many. His legacy has inspired generations to continue his quest for a world without cancer.

The Discovery of Insulin

The discovery of insulin is a landmark moment in the history of medicine that revolutionized the treatment of diabetes. It was a collaborative effort led by Frederick Banting, Charles Best, James Collip, and John Macleod, and their breakthrough occurred in the early 1920s.

At the time, diabetes was a serious and often deadly disease with no effective treatment. Patients with type 1 diabetes relied on strict dietary restrictions and faced a grim prognosis. Banting, a Canadian physician, became determined to find a solution and focused his research on the pancreas, believing it played a crucial role in diabetes.

Banting approached Macleod, a professor of physiology at the University of Toronto, who provided him with a laboratory and resources. Banting also enlisted the help of Charles Best, a medical student, as his assistant. Together, they began their experiments.

Their breakthrough came in 1921 when Banting and Best successfully extracted insulin from the pancreas of dogs and demonstrated its ability to regulate blood sugar levels. The discovery was a turning point in the understanding and treatment of diabetes. It opened up new possibilities for managing the disease and gave hope to millions of people worldwide.

Banting and Best's findings attracted significant attention, and with the assistance of James Collip, a biochemist, they were able to refine and purify the insulin extract for human use. In 1922, the first successful injection of insulin was administered to a young boy with diabetes, Leonard Thompson. The results were remarkable, as his condition improved dramatically.

News of the discovery spread rapidly, and insulin became widely available as a life-saving treatment for diabetes. Banting and Macleod were awarded the Nobel Prize in Physiology or Medicine in 1923 for their ground-breaking work, though Banting shared his prize money with Best, acknowledging his crucial contribution.

The discovery of insulin not only transformed the lives of individuals with diabetes but also laid the foundation for further research and advancements in the field of endocrinology. It sparked ongoing efforts to improve insulin therapy, develop different insulin formulations, and explore alternative treatments for diabetes.

Today, insulin remains a vital medication for managing diabetes, and its discovery stands as a testament to the power of scientific collaboration, innovation, and the relentless pursuit of solutions to improve human health. The impact of the discovery of insulin cannot be overstated, as it continues to save and enhance countless lives worldwide.

The Tragically Hip

The Tragically Hip, often referred to as simply The Hip, is a Canadian rock band that achieved significant success and acclaim both in their home country and internationally. Formed in Kingston, Ontario in 1984, the band consisted of lead vocalist Gord Downie, guitarists Rob Baker and Paul Langlois, bassist Gord Sinclair, and drummer Johnny Fay.

Known for their distinctive sound and poetic lyrics, The Tragically Hip's music defies easy categorization. Their style blends elements of rock, alternative, and blues, with introspective and often politically charged lyrics. The band's music resonates deeply with Canadian audiences, capturing the essence of the country's cultural identity and experiences.

Throughout their career, The Tragically Hip released numerous albums, with several of them becoming commercial and critical successes. Their 1989 album "Up to Here" featuring hits like "New Orleans Is Sinking" and "Blow at High Dough" marked their breakthrough, earning them a dedicated following.

One of the defining aspects of The Tragically Hip's career is their incredible live performances. They are renowned for their dynamic and energetic shows, with Gord Downie's charismatic stage presence captivating audiences. The band's live performances have become legendary in Canada, with their concerts often selling out and drawing massive crowds.

Despite their success in Canada, The Tragically Hip did not achieve the same level of mainstream recognition internationally. However, their influence on Canadian music and their status as cultural icons cannot be overstated. They have been praised for their poetic lyrics, thought-provoking themes, and their ability to capture the essence of the Canadian experience.

In 2016, The Tragically Hip embarked on what would be their final tour after Gord Downie was diagnosed with terminal brain cancer. The tour, appropriately named the "Man Machine Poem Tour," became a deeply emotional and poignant farewell to their fans. The final concert, held in their hometown of Kingston, was broadcast live and watched by millions across Canada, solidifying their status as national treasures.

The Tragically Hip's legacy extends beyond their music. They have been recognized for their social and political activism, using their platform to raise awareness and support various causes. Gord Downie's diagnosis and subsequent advocacy for Indigenous rights and reconciliation with Canada's Indigenous peoples further cemented their impact and influence.

The Tragically Hip's music continues to resonate with fans old and new, and their songs remain beloved anthems in Canada. Their poetic storytelling and evocative melodies have left an indelible mark on Canadian music history, ensuring their place as one of the most iconic and influential rock bands in the country.

The Montreal Olympics

The Montreal Olympics, officially known as the Games of the XXI Olympiad, were held in Montreal, Canada, from July 17 to August 1, 1976. It was a significant event in Olympic history, showcasing not only athletic excellence but also facing numerous challenges and leaving a lasting impact on the host city.

The Montreal Olympics was marked by several notable achievements and memorable moments. One of the standout performances was by Romanian gymnast Nadia Comaneci, who became the first gymnast in Olympic history to score a perfect 10.0, accomplishing the feat seven times during the competition. Comaneci's extraordinary performances captured the world's attention and established her as a gymnastics legend.

Another historic moment of the Montreal Olympics was the participation of South Africa. The country's apartheid policies led to its exclusion from the Olympics since 1964, but under pressure, the International Olympic Committee (IOC) allowed South Africa to compete again. However, this decision resulted in several African countries boycotting the Games in protest.

The Montreal Olympics faced significant financial challenges, with cost overruns and construction delays leading to a substantial debt burden for the host city. The event's infrastructure, particularly the iconic Olympic Stadium with its retractable roof, faced numerous issues and ultimately became a symbol of the financial difficulties encountered during the Games.

Despite the challenges, the Montreal Olympics left a lasting legacy. The event showcased Canada's ability to host a major international sporting event and introduced several innovative elements, such as the first Olympic mascot, Amik the beaver, and the introduction of electronic timing devices for swimming events.

The Montreal Olympics also had a positive impact on the city's infrastructure and sports facilities. The construction of Olympic venues, including the Olympic Park and the Olympic Village, revitalized the city's urban landscape and provided new sports facilities that continue to be used today.

Moreover, the Montreal Olympics had a cultural impact on the city. The Games featured an array of cultural events and celebrations, including art exhibitions, concerts, and performances, promoting the diversity and artistic richness of Montreal and Canada as a whole.

In terms of athletic achievements, the United States topped the medal table with 34 gold medals, followed by the Soviet Union with 49 gold medals. The Games showcased impressive performances from athletes across various sports disciplines, highlighting their dedication, skill, and determination.

The Montreal Olympics holds a place in Olympic history as a complex and challenging event, marred by financial difficulties but also marked by memorable moments and significant athletic achievements. It remains a reminder of the immense undertaking and impact of hosting the Olympic Games, both on the sporting world and the host city.

The Rescue of the Halifax Explosion Survivors

The Halifax Explosion, which occurred on December 6, 1917, was a devastating maritime disaster that resulted from the collision of two ships in the Halifax Harbor in Nova Scotia, Canada. The explosion caused widespread destruction, with a significant loss of life and extensive damage to the city. In the aftermath of the explosion, a remarkable rescue effort took place to save survivors and provide them with medical assistance, shelter, and support.

The immediate impact of the explosion was catastrophic. The blast wave and subsequent fires destroyed buildings, ships, and infrastructure in the area, causing widespread chaos and confusion. Thousands of people were injured, and many were trapped under debris or in collapsed structures. The situation called for a swift and coordinated response to rescue survivors and provide aid to the affected population.

The rescue efforts were led by a combination of professional emergency responders, including firefighters, police officers, and medical personnel, as well as ordinary citizens who volunteered their time and resources to assist in the rescue and recovery operations. The response was a testament to the resilience and solidarity of the Halifax community in the face of overwhelming adversity.

Local hospitals were quickly overwhelmed by the influx of injured individuals, prompting the establishment of temporary medical facilities to treat the wounded. Medical personnel worked tirelessly to provide critical care and save lives, often under challenging conditions and with limited resources.

The Canadian and American military also played a significant role in the rescue efforts. The Royal Canadian Navy and the United States Navy dispatched ships to the area to assist with evacuation, provide medical aid, and transport injured individuals to nearby hospitals. The military personnel worked alongside civilian volunteers, utilizing their training and resources to help save lives.

Volunteer organizations, such as the Red Cross, provided essential support in the aftermath of the explosion. They set up emergency shelters, distributed food and supplies, and offered assistance to those who had lost their homes and belongings. The outpouring of support from both local and international organizations and individuals helped to alleviate the suffering and provide much-needed comfort to the survivors.

The rescue and relief efforts continued for weeks and months following the explosion, as the city worked to rebuild and recover from the devastation. The Halifax Explosion remains one of the largest non-nuclear explosions in history, but the heroic efforts of the rescue teams and the support of the community ensured that many lives were saved and that the survivors received the care and assistance they needed.

The rescue of the Halifax Explosion survivors stands as a testament to the power of collective action and compassion in times of crisis. The response of emergency responders, medical professionals, military personnel, and volunteers showcased the strength and resilience of the human spirit. The efforts made during this tragedy continue to inspire and remind us of the importance of unity and solidarity in times of need.

The Birth of Greenpeace

The birth of Greenpeace marked a significant turning point in the global environmental movement. In the early 1970s, a group of activists and ecologists came together to form an organization that would raise awareness about environmental issues and advocate for positive change. The founders of Greenpeace were motivated by their deep concern for the environment and the urgent need to address pressing environmental problems.

The origins of Greenpeace can be traced back to Vancouver, Canada, in 1971. A small group of activists, including Irving Stowe, Dorothy Stowe, Ben Metcalfe, Marie Bohlen, Bob Hunter, and Bob Cummings, joined forces to protest against US nuclear weapons testing in Alaska's Amchitka Island. They believed that the nuclear tests posed a significant threat to the environment and wanted to take a stand against them.

On September 15, 1971, the group set sail on a fishing boat named the Phyllis Cormack towards the test site. They intended to disrupt the nuclear tests and draw attention to the dangers they posed. Although they did not reach Amchitka Island, their journey garnered significant media attention and sparked a wave of public support for their cause.

Following the voyage, the group officially named themselves "Greenpeace" and began to focus on a wide range of environmental issues. They adopted the symbol of a rainbow-colored peace sign, which became synonymous with the organization. Greenpeace rapidly gained momentum and attracted activists and supporters from around the world.

One of Greenpeace's earliest campaigns centered around the

conservation of whales. In 1975, the organization launched its first direct-action campaign against commercial whaling. Activists sailed into the path of whaling ships to disrupt their operations and document the cruel treatment of whales. This campaign helped to raise global awareness about the plight of these magnificent creatures and led to a ban on commercial whaling in many countries.

Greenpeace's activism extended to other pressing environmental issues, including deforestation, pollution, climate change, and the protection of endangered species. The organization gained a reputation for its direct-action approach, using peaceful protests, nonviolent civil disobedience, and high-profile campaigns to draw attention to environmental degradation and push for policy changes.

Over the years, Greenpeace has grown into one of the world's most influential environmental organizations. It has expanded its operations to numerous countries and continues to play a vital role in advocating for environmental conservation and sustainability. Greenpeace's work has inspired millions of individuals to take action, raise their voices, and work towards a more sustainable and equitable future for the planet.

The birth of Greenpeace marked a turning point in the history of environmental activism. It demonstrated the power of grassroots movements and collective action in driving positive change. Greenpeace's unwavering commitment to protecting the environment has had a lasting impact on the global environmental movement and serves as an inspiration for future generations to stand up for the planet.

The Canadian Space Program

The Canadian Space Program is a significant national endeavor that encompasses Canada's involvement in space exploration, satellite communications, scientific research, and technology development. While Canada does not have its own human spaceflight program, it has made significant contributions to space exploration through collaborations with international partners, particularly the United States.

The Canadian Space Program has its roots in the establishment of the National Research Council (NRC) in 1916, which played a crucial role in fostering scientific research and development in the country. In the 1960s, Canada started focusing on space-related activities with the launch of its first satellite, Alouette 1, in 1962. This marked Canada's entry into the space age and laid the foundation for its subsequent achievements.

In the early 1980s, Canada made a landmark contribution to the space shuttle program with the development of the Canadarm robotic manipulator system. The Canadarm, known officially as the Shuttle Remote Manipulator System (SRMS), was a robotic arm used on the space shuttle to deploy and retrieve satellites, assist in spacewalks, and perform various tasks in space. The success of the Canadarm established Canada as a key player in space robotics and set the stage for future collaborations.

Another major milestone for the Canadian Space Program came in 1989 with the launch of the first Canadian communication satellite, Anik C1. This marked Canada's entry into the field of satellite communications, providing the country with improved telecommunications capabilities and paving the way for future advancements in satellite technology.

In recent years, Canada has continued to play an active role in space exploration and scientific research through its participation in international missions. One notable example is Canada's contribution to the International Space Station (ISS) program. Canada provided the ISS with its iconic robotic systems, including the Canadarm2 and the Dextre robotic hand, which have been vital for assembly, maintenance, and scientific experiments on the space station.

Canada has also been involved in various space science missions, including the RADARSAT series of Earth observation satellites, which have contributed to monitoring and managing Canada's vast and diverse territory. Additionally, Canada has made significant contributions to space astronomy through its involvement in missions such as the James Webb Space Telescope and the Hubble Space Telescope.

The Canadian Space Agency (CSA) is the primary organization responsible for coordinating Canada's activities in space. Established in 1989, the CSA oversees the country's space policy, promotes space science and research, supports the development of space technologies, and fosters international collaborations. The agency works closely with Canadian industry, academia, and international partners to advance Canada's capabilities and contributions in space.

The Canadian Space Program has not only enabled scientific discoveries and technological advancements but has also inspired generations of Canadians to pursue careers in science, technology, engineering, and mathematics (STEM). It has fostered innovation, economic growth, and international collaboration while positioning Canada as a respected player in the global space community.

As Canada looks to the future, it continues to explore opportunities for further advancements in space technology, satellite communications, Earth observation, and participation in international space missions. The Canadian Space Program remains a symbol of the country's dedication to scientific exploration, innovation, and its aspiration to contribute to the understanding of our universe.

The Quiet Revolution

The Quiet Revolution refers to a period of significant social, cultural, and political change that took place in the Canadian province of Quebec during the 1960s. It marked a transformative shift in the province's society, economy, and governance, leading to a more secular, modern, and assertive Quebec.

The Quiet Revolution was characterized by a desire for change and a break from traditional societal norms and institutions. It emerged as a response to the perceived stagnation, conservatism, and dominance of the Roman Catholic Church in Quebec, as well as economic disparities and political discontent.

One of the key aspects of the Quiet Revolution was the secularization of Quebec society. The influence of the Catholic Church diminished significantly as the province embraced a more secular outlook. This led to reforms such as the legalization of divorce, the liberalization of abortion laws, and the removal of religious symbols from public institutions. The government also introduced a secular education system, reducing the role of the Church in public schools.

The Quiet Revolution also focused on modernizing Quebec's economy and expanding the role of the state. The government implemented various economic policies aimed at diversifying and strengthening the province's industries, including the nationalization of hydroelectric resources and the creation of government-owned corporations. This economic intervention by the state aimed to foster growth, increase employment opportunities, and reduce dependence on traditional industries.

Politically, the Quiet Revolution saw the rise of a more assertive and nationalist Quebec. The provincial government, led by Premier Jean Lesage, implemented a series of reforms known as the "Lesage Revolution." These reforms aimed to centralize power in the provincial government, increase autonomy from the federal government, and promote the French language and culture.

The Quiet Revolution also had significant implications for Quebec's relationship with the rest of Canada. It sparked a renewed sense of identity and pride among Quebecois, leading to the emergence of Quebec nationalism and calls for greater self-determination. This ultimately led to the rise of the separatist movement and the formation of the Parti Québécois, a political party advocating for Quebec's independence from Canada.

The Quiet Revolution had a lasting impact on Quebec and shaped its modern identity. It transformed the province socially, politically, and economically, paving the way for a more secular, progressive, and self-confident Quebec. While the Quiet Revolution was not without controversy and challenges, it remains a defining period in Quebec's history and continues to shape the province's social, cultural, and political landscape to this day.

The Canadian Charter of Rights and Freedoms

The Canadian Charter of Rights and Freedoms, often referred to simply as the Charter, is a constitutional document that forms a vital part of Canada's Constitution. Enacted in 1982, the Charter sets out the fundamental rights and freedoms of individuals in Canada and protects them from infringement by government authorities.

The Charter guarantees a wide range of rights and freedoms, including fundamental freedoms such as freedom of expression, freedom of religion, freedom of assembly, and freedom of association. It also protects democratic rights, such as the right to vote and the right to participate in political activities. The Charter further ensures mobility rights, which guarantee that Canadian citizens can move freely within the country and establish residence in any province or territory.

One of the key aspects of the Charter is its protection of equality rights. It prohibits discrimination on various grounds, including race, national or ethnic origin, religion, gender, age, and more. This provision ensures that all individuals are treated equally under the law and have the right to equal protection and benefit without discrimination.

The Charter also includes legal rights, which provide individuals with safeguards when involved in legal proceedings. These rights include the right to be informed promptly of the reasons for arrest or detention, the right to legal counsel, the right to a fair trial, and protection against cruel and unusual punishment.

Notably, the Charter contains a clause known as the "notwithstanding clause" or Section 33. This provision allows the federal and provincial governments to temporarily override certain rights and freedoms outlined in the Charter, but it has limitations and is subject to judicial review.

The introduction of the Charter has had a profound impact on Canadian society. It has shaped legal and social discourse, informed court decisions, and played a crucial role in protecting individual rights and promoting equality. The Charter has become a symbol of Canada's commitment to human rights and has set a standard for democratic societies around the world.

The Creation of Universal Healthcare

The creation of universal healthcare in Canada is a significant milestone in the country's history and has had a profound impact on the well-being of its citizens. Universal healthcare, also known as medicare, refers to a healthcare system that provides essential medical services to all residents regardless of their ability to pay.

In Canada, the establishment of universal healthcare can be traced back to the efforts of Tommy Douglas, a prominent political figure and the premier of Saskatchewan in the 1940s and 1950s. Douglas, along with his government, implemented a pioneering healthcare program in Saskatchewan called the Saskatchewan Hospital Services Plan. This plan provided comprehensive medical coverage to all residents of the province.

The success of the Saskatchewan program led to the introduction of the federal Medical Care Act in 1966, under the leadership of Prime Minister Lester B. Pearson. The act provided federal funding to provincial and territorial governments that implemented universal healthcare programs. Over time, all provinces and territories in Canada adopted their own healthcare systems, guided by the principles of universality, accessibility, comprehensiveness, portability, and public administration.

Under the Canadian healthcare system, residents have access to medically necessary hospital services, physician services, and many other healthcare services, including preventative care, diagnostic tests, and prescription medications. The costs of these services are primarily covered through taxes and government funding.

The creation of universal healthcare in Canada has had numerous benefits. It ensures that all Canadians have access to essential healthcare services, regardless of their income or social status. It promotes equal treatment and helps reduce disparities in health outcomes. It also provides financial protection by reducing or eliminating the need for individuals to pay out-of-pocket for medical expenses.

However, the Canadian healthcare system also faces challenges, such as long wait times for certain procedures and shortages of healthcare professionals in certain regions. Efforts are continuously being made to address these issues and improve the system to meet the evolving healthcare needs of Canadians.

Overall, the creation of universal healthcare in Canada represents a commitment to providing equitable healthcare services to all residents, and it remains an integral part of the country's identity and values.

The National Inquiry into Missing and Murdered Indigenous Women and Girls

The National Inquiry into Missing and Murdered Indigenous Women and Girls (MMIWG) was a significant and long-overdue initiative in Canada aimed at addressing the systemic violence and discrimination faced by Indigenous women, girls, and Two-Spirit individuals. The inquiry was officially launched in September 2016 and concluded with the release of its final report in June 2019.

The inquiry was established in response to the alarming rates of violence and the disproportionate number of missing and murdered Indigenous women and girls in Canada. It sought to shed light on the root causes of this violence, examine the systemic failures in the justice system, and provide recommendations for meaningful change and reconciliation.

Throughout its duration, the inquiry heard testimonies from thousands of family members, survivors, and experts, who shared their personal stories and experiences. The voices of Indigenous communities and their lived realities were central to the inquiry's work, ensuring that their perspectives were heard and honored.

The inquiry's final report, titled "Reclaiming Power and Place," painted a disturbing picture of the pervasive violence, discrimination, and marginalization experienced by Indigenous women, girls, and Two-Spirit individuals. It highlighted the interconnectedness of colonialism, racism, sexism, and other forms of oppression that contribute to the high rates of violence against Indigenous women.

The report made numerous recommendations addressing various areas, including justice, health, social services, education, and media representation. These recommendations aimed to address the underlying factors contributing to the violence, improve support services for victims and their families, enhance police investigations, and promote Indigenous-led initiatives and solutions.

The inquiry played a crucial role in raising awareness about the issue of missing and murdered Indigenous women and girls, challenging societal attitudes, and urging the government and institutions to take action. It brought attention to the need for a comprehensive and coordinated response to address the ongoing violence and systemic issues faced by Indigenous communities.

However, it is important to note that the work does not end with the inquiry. The implementation of the report's recommendations, along with continued efforts to support Indigenous communities, address root causes, and promote healing and reconciliation, remains an ongoing responsibility for all levels of government, institutions, and society as a whole.

The National Inquiry into Missing and Murdered Indigenous Women and Girls served as a pivotal moment in Canadian history, highlighting the urgent need for justice, equality, and the recognition of Indigenous rights. It represented an important step toward healing, truth-telling, and creating a more inclusive and just society for all.

The Winnipeg General Strike

The Winnipeg General Strike was a landmark event in Canadian labor history that occurred in Winnipeg, Manitoba, in 1919. It was a massive and unprecedented labor protest that involved thousands of workers from various industries demanding better working conditions, higher wages, and the right to collective bargaining.

The strike began on May 15, 1919, when metalworkers walked off the job after negotiations between their union and employers failed. The strike quickly spread to other sectors, including building and construction trades, transportation, and public services. Within days, over 30,000 workers, both unionized and non-unionized, joined the strike, effectively shutting down the city.

The workers' demands were fueled by poor working conditions, low wages, long hours, and a lack of job security. They were also inspired by the success of labor movements in other parts of the world, such as the Russian Revolution and the labor unrest in Europe and the United States.

The strike garnered significant support from the community, with many residents participating in solidarity rallies and demonstrations. However, the strike was met with strong opposition from business leaders, the government, and conservative elements in society who feared the growing influence of the labor movement.

Tensions escalated on June 21, 1919, when a confrontation between striking workers and the Royal Northwest Mounted Police (RNWMP) resulted in violence and the death of two strikers.

This event, known as "Bloody Saturday," marked a turning point in the strike and led to its eventual end.

The strike officially ended on June 26, 1919, after the strike committee called off the protest to prevent further violence and allow for negotiations. While the immediate demands of the workers were not fully met, the strike had a profound impact on Canadian labor rights and shaped the future of the labor movement in the country.

The Winnipeg General Strike brought issues of workers' rights, social justice, and income inequality to the forefront of public consciousness. It led to the formation of new unions, the rise of socialist and labor movements, and significant changes in labor legislation across Canada.

Although the strike was suppressed and many strike leaders faced persecution and blacklisting, its legacy remains as a symbol of worker solidarity and the fight for fair and equitable working conditions. The Winnipeg General Strike serves as a powerful reminder of the ongoing struggle for labor rights and social justice in Canada.

The Creation of Cirque du Soleil

The creation of Cirque du Soleil is a remarkable tale of creativity, innovation, and the fusion of various artistic disciplines. What began as a small group of street performers in Quebec, Canada, has evolved into a global phenomenon that has redefined the world of circus arts.

In the early 1980s, a group of talented street performers, led by Guy Laliberté, came together with a vision to create a unique form of entertainment that would challenge the conventions of traditional circus. They wanted to blend circus acts with theatrical elements, music, dance, and storytelling to create a mesmerizing and immersive experience for the audience.

With a shared passion for pushing artistic boundaries, the founding members of Cirque du Soleil embarked on their creative journey. They combined traditional circus skills such as acrobatics, juggling, and contortion with innovative staging, imaginative costumes, and original music compositions. They rejected the use of animals in their performances, focusing instead on the incredible capabilities of human performers.

The first Cirque du Soleil show, "Le Grand Tour du Cirque du Soleil," premiered in 1984 and immediately captured the attention and imagination of audiences. The troupe's innovative approach to circus arts, characterized by a fusion of artistry, athleticism, and storytelling, struck a chord with people around the world.

Cirque du Soleil continued to innovate and expand, creating new shows and touring internationally. They introduced groundbreaking techniques like the use of bungee cords, aerial harnesses, and elaborate sets to enhance the visual spectacle of their performances. Each show told a unique story, taking the audience on a journey of imagination and wonder.

The success of Cirque du Soleil can be attributed not only to its awe-inspiring performances but also to its commitment to artistic excellence, creativity, and collaboration. The company brought together a diverse team of performers, musicians, designers, and technicians from around the world, fostering a collaborative environment where ideas could flourish.

Over the years, Cirque du Soleil has become synonymous with innovation, pushing the boundaries of what is possible in live entertainment. Its shows have delighted millions of spectators worldwide, captivating them with their extraordinary feats of human skill, breathtaking visuals, and emotional storytelling.

The creation of Cirque du Soleil stands as a testament to the power of imagination and the transformative impact of the arts. It has inspired countless artists and performers and continues to captivate audiences with its unparalleled blend of artistry, athleticism, and sheer spectacle. Cirque du Soleil has truly revolutionized the world of circus and has left an indelible mark on the global entertainment landscape.

The Avro Arrow

The Avro Arrow remains one of Canada's most iconic and controversial projects in aerospace history. Developed by the A.V. Roe Canada (Avro) company in the late 1950s, the Avro Arrow was an advanced supersonic interceptor aircraft designed to defend Canadian airspace during the Cold War.

The development of the Avro Arrow was a significant achievement for Canada, as it showcased the country's engineering and technological capabilities. The aircraft featured several groundbreaking innovations, including delta wings, a fly-by-wire control system, and a powerful engine capable of reaching speeds exceeding Mach 2. Its sleek design and cutting-edge technology positioned the Avro Arrow among the most advanced aircraft of its time.

The Avro Arrow was more than just an aircraft; it symbolized Canada's ambition to establish itself as a leader in aerospace technology. The project garnered widespread national pride and showcased Canada's potential in the global aerospace industry. However, the program faced numerous challenges, including escalating costs and changing geopolitical dynamics.

Despite its promising start, the Avro Arrow's fate took a sudden turn in 1959 when the Canadian government abruptly canceled the program. The decision was met with shock and disappointment, as it meant the end of an ambitious venture that many believed would propel Canada to the forefront of aerospace technology. The cancellation resulted in the loss of highly skilled jobs and the destruction of the existing aircraft and production facilities, leaving a void in Canada's aerospace industry.

The reasons behind the cancellation of the Avro Arrow project are still debated today. Some argue that cost overruns and changing defense priorities led to the decision, while others believe political pressures and external influences played a significant role. Regardless of the reasons, the cancellation of the Avro Arrow had a profound impact on Canada's aerospace industry and its national identity.

The legacy of the Avro Arrow lives on in Canadian history and culture. It continues to be a symbol of technological excellence, national pride, and the potential for Canada to compete on a global scale. The story of the Avro Arrow serves as a reminder of the challenges faced by ambitious projects and the complex intersection of politics, economics, and national priorities.

Today, the Avro Arrow is remembered through various exhibitions, museums, and memorials that honor its significance in Canadian aviation history. The aircraft's legacy also fuels ongoing discussions about Canada's role in the aerospace industry and the importance of supporting domestic technological advancements.

In conclusion, the Avro Arrow remains a symbol of Canada's ambitious pursuit of aerospace technology and its desire to establish a national identity in a rapidly changing world. While the project's cancellation was met with disappointment, the Avro Arrow continues to hold a special place in Canadian history, reminding us of the country's technological achievements and the challenges faced in the pursuit of greatness.

The Battle of Vimy Ridge

The Battle of Vimy Ridge, which took place during World War I from April 9 to April 12, 1917, was a significant event in Canadian military history and played a crucial role in shaping Canada's national identity. It was part of the larger Battle of Arras, fought between the Allied forces, primarily composed of British and Canadian troops, and the German Empire.

Vimy Ridge, located in northern France, was a strategic high ground that had been heavily fortified by the Germans. Previous attempts by other Allied forces to capture the ridge had been unsuccessful, resulting in significant casualties. However, the Canadian Corps, consisting of four Canadian divisions fighting together for the first time, was given the task of capturing Vimy Ridge.

Under the command of General Arthur Currie, the Canadian Corps meticulously planned and prepared for the assault on Vimy Ridge. They employed innovative tactics and techniques, including extensive reconnaissance, the use of artillery, and the introduction of creeping barrages, to overcome the challenges presented by the heavily fortified German positions.

On the morning of April 9, 1917, the Canadian troops launched their attack. Despite facing fierce opposition and intense German counterattacks, they displayed remarkable bravery, determination, and exceptional teamwork. The Canadian Corps successfully captured the ridge within a matter of days, achieving a significant victory that had eluded previous attempts by other Allied forces.

The success at Vimy Ridge was attributed to several key

factors. The meticulous planning, effective use of artillery, and the integration of infantry, artillery, and engineering units allowed the Canadian troops to overcome the formidable German defenses. Moreover, the Canadian soldiers demonstrated exceptional discipline, courage, and resilience in the face of adversity.

The Battle of Vimy Ridge was a turning point for Canada. It marked the first time that all four divisions of the Canadian Corps fought together as a unified force, and their success bolstered Canada's reputation as a formidable fighting force on the world stage. The battle also came to symbolize Canada's coming of age and its emergence as a nation separate from its British colonial roots.

The significance of the Battle of Vimy Ridge extends beyond its military achievements. It is often seen as a defining moment in Canadian history, representing the sacrifices made by Canadian soldiers and their contributions to the Allied victory in World War I. The battle is commemorated annually in Canada on April 9th as Vimy Ridge Day, honoring the courage and valor of those who fought and paid the ultimate price.

Today, the Vimy Memorial stands as a solemn tribute to the Canadian soldiers who fought and died during the battle. Located on the ridge itself, the memorial serves as a reminder of the sacrifices made and the enduring legacy of the Battle of Vimy Ridge.

In conclusion, the Battle of Vimy Ridge was a pivotal moment in Canadian history, showcasing the bravery and skill of Canadian soldiers and solidifying Canada's national identity. It remains a testament to the courage and sacrifice of those who fought and serves as a symbol of the country's military achievements.

The Iditarod Dog Sled Race

The Iditarod Dog Sled Race is an iconic and grueling long-distance sled dog race that takes place annually in Alaska, United States. It is considered one of the most challenging and prestigious sled dog races in the world, spanning over 1,000 miles (1,600 kilometers) of rugged terrain, harsh weather conditions, and remote wilderness.

The race is named after the Iditarod Trail, a historic dogsled route that was used in the early 20th century for transportation and delivering supplies to remote Alaskan communities. The Iditarod Trail became famous during the 1925 serum run to Nome when a relay of dog teams delivered life-saving diphtheria antitoxin to the town, preventing a potential epidemic.

The first Iditarod race was held in 1973 to commemorate the historic Iditarod Trail and the role of sled dogs in Alaskan history. Today, the race attracts mushers from around the world who compete for the title of Iditarod champion. Mushers, accompanied by their team of highly trained sled dogs, face extreme challenges as they traverse treacherous mountain ranges, frozen rivers, dense forests, and the unpredictable Alaskan wilderness.

The race typically begins on the first Saturday in March in Anchorage and finishes in Nome, with checkpoints along the way where mushers rest, care for their dogs, and replenish supplies. Mushers must navigate through blizzards, sub-zero temperatures, and treacherous terrain, relying on their navigation skills and the endurance and strength of their canine companions.

The Iditarod is not just a test of physical strength and endurance but also a celebration of the deep bond between mushers and their dogs. The teams rely on each other for survival, with mushers relying on the dogs' instincts, athleticism, and resilience to overcome the challenges of the race. The dogs, in turn, depend on the musher for guidance, care, and support throughout the journey.

The Iditarod is not without controversy, as concerns have been raised about the treatment and welfare of the dogs during the race. In response, numerous regulations and protocols have been implemented to ensure the well-being and safety of the canine athletes. Veterinarians stationed at checkpoints along the trail closely monitor the health of the dogs, and any signs of fatigue, injury, or illness prompt immediate intervention.

The Iditarod Dog Sled Race captures the imagination of people worldwide and is a significant cultural event in Alaska. It showcases the indomitable spirit, determination, and bond between humans and animals. The race also serves as a platform to promote and preserve the rich history and traditions of sled dog mushing in Alaska.

In conclusion, the Iditarod Dog Sled Race is a remarkable and challenging event that honors the legacy of the Iditarod Trail and the crucial role of sled dogs in Alaska's history. It is a testament to the endurance, skill, and partnership between mushers and their dogs, as they brave the elements and conquer the unforgiving Alaskan wilderness. The Iditarod continues to captivate and inspire people worldwide, showcasing the extraordinary bond between humans and animals in the pursuit of a shared goal.

As we come to the end of "Great Canadian Chronicles: Extraordinary Tales of Resilience, Innovation, and Heritage," we reflect on the remarkable journey we have embarked upon through the stories that define Canada. From coast to coast, we have explored the narratives of resilience, the triumphs of innovation, and the preservation of heritage that make Canada a truly exceptional nation.

Throughout this book, we have encountered individuals who faced adversity head-on and overcame it with unwavering determination. From the valiant explorers who ventured into uncharted territories to the trailblazers who challenged societal norms, each story showcases the indomitable spirit of Canadians.

The innovations born on Canadian soil have changed the world in significant ways. From ground-breaking technological advancements to transformative discoveries in various fields, Canada has been at the forefront of innovation. We have celebrated the contributions of inventors, scientists, and visionaries who have left an indelible mark on human progress.

Moreover, Canada's rich and diverse heritage has been a source of strength and unity. We have explored the cultural tapestry woven by Indigenous communities, immigrant populations, and generations of Canadians who have preserved their traditions and enriched the nation's identity. The celebration of heritage and the embrace of multiculturalism have made Canada a beacon of inclusivity and understanding.

As we conclude our journey through the Great Canadian Chronicles, let us be inspired by the tales of resilience, innovation, and heritage that we have encountered. May these stories ignite our own spirit of perseverance, fuel our creative endeavors, and deepen our appreciation for the diverse cultures that make up the fabric of Canada.

We hope that this book has provided you with a newfound appreciation for the remarkable achievements and stories that have shaped Canada. Let the Great Canadian Chronicles serve as a reminder of the incredible potential that lies within us all and the power of resilience, innovation, and heritage to shape the future.

Thank you for joining us on this extraordinary exploration of Canada's past, present, and future. We encourage you to continue seeking out the remarkable tales that lie within every corner of this great nation, and may you be inspired to contribute your own chapter to the ongoing chronicles of Canada's resilience, innovation, and heritage.